Look at them Go

Written by Catherine Coe

Collins

Pull the car back.

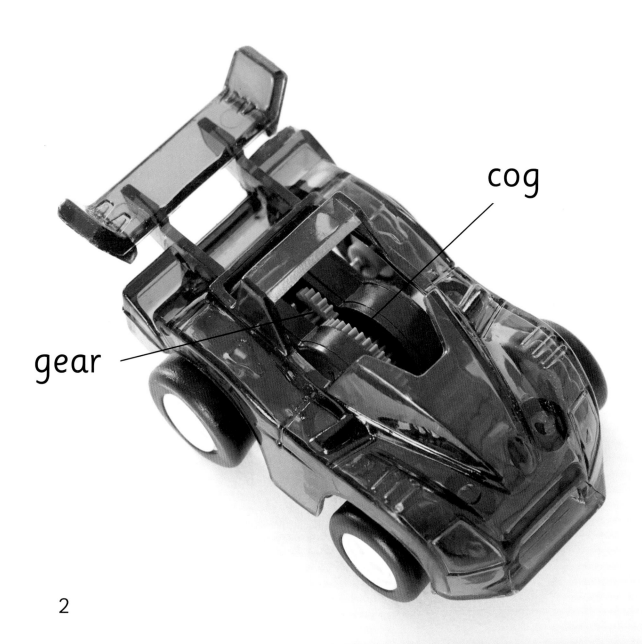

cog

gear

Off it zooms!

Push it down.

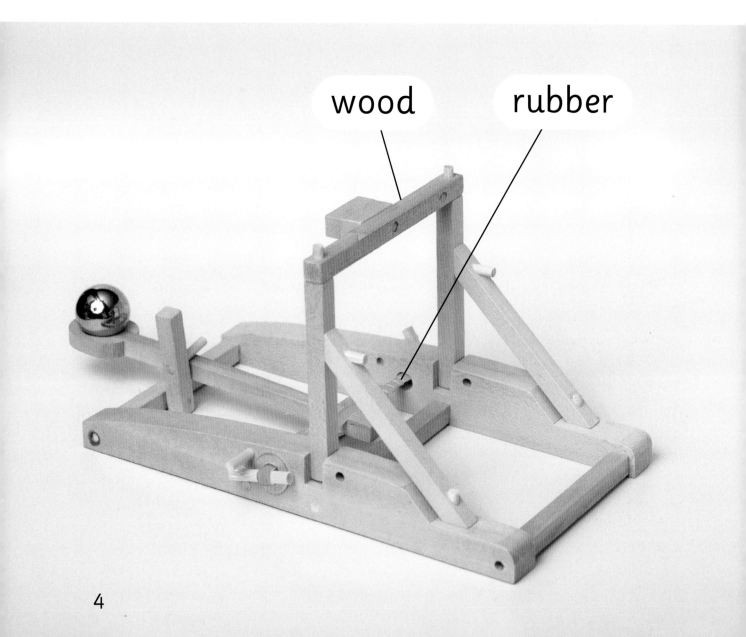

wood

rubber

Off it pops!

See cogs turn.

gears

cogs

Look at it go!

Push the button in.

button

It shoots!

Push the pedal.

pedal

The pedal turns the chain.

chain

Fill the balloon with hot air.

hot air

It zooms up!

Off they go!

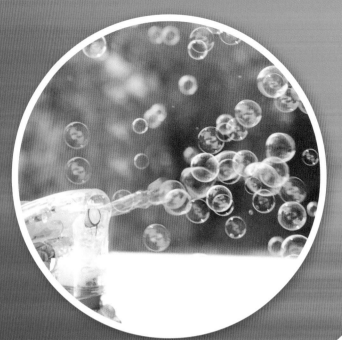

Letters and Sounds: Phase 3

Word count: 60

Focus phonemes: /ar/ /oo/ /ow/ /ear/ /er/ /oo/ /ee/ /ur/ /ai/ /air/ tt, bb

Common exception words: pull, the, push, go, they

Curriculum links: Mathematics: Numbers Shape, space and measures

Early learning goals: Listening and attention: children listen attentively in a range of situations; Understanding: answer 'how' and 'why' questions about their experiences and in response to stories or events; Reading: read and understand simple sentences, use phonic knowledge to decode regular words and read them aloud accurately, read some common irregular words

Developing fluency

- Your child may enjoy hearing you read the story.
- You could read the even number pages (e.g. page 2: Pull the car back.) to your child and ask them to read the odd number pages (e.g. page 3: Off it zooms!), with lots of expression.

Phonic practice

- Point to the word **button** on page 8 and talk about the /t/ sound represented by 'tt'. Model sounding out the word and then blending the sounds together. Ask your child to copy you. Do the same with the following words:

rubber   off   balloon

Extending vocabulary

- Flick through the book again, pointing at the words on pages 3, 5, 7, 9, 11, 13 that describe how each thing 'goes'. Model reading the words, such as **zooms** with lots of exaggeration, using your voice to make the sound. Encourage your child to make the sounds with their voice e.g. **zooms, pops, shoots**. Can they think of any other sound words to describe the pictures (e.g. *tick, tock* or *ring* on page 7)?
- Look at page 2 with your child. Point to the labels and model reading them. Talk about how labels give us more information about the picture. Ask your child if there is any other part of the car we could add a label to (e.g. *wheel*).
- Now do the same for page 10 (e.g. *wheel, seat, tyre, handles*) and page 12 (e.g. *basket, people, rope, fire*).